PRAIS
THE IDE

"Those few milliseconds of a working life in which you somehow see your world in a wholly new light are infinitely more valuable than the many hours we all spend churning through inconsequential emails. Unfortunately there is no surefire way of generating these priceless moments. Books such as this one, however, will significantly improve your odds."

RORY SUTHERLAND
Vice Chairman, Ogilvy UK

"Throughout, Kevin's belief that good ideas are available to anyone willing to put in the necessary levels of preparation and diligence, as opposed to the divine right of a few enlightened individuals, shines like a beacon. Invaluable."

CHRIS CARMICHAEL
Director Media & Digital Marketing, EMEA, Hewlett-Packard

Published by
LID Publishing
An imprint of LID Business Media Ltd.
LABS House, 15-19 Bloomsbury Way,
London, WC1A 2TH, UK

info@lidpublishing.com
www.lidpublishing.com

A member of:

businesspublishersroundtable.com

© Kevin Duncan, 2022
© LID Business Media Limited, 2022

Printed by Imak Ofset

ISBN: 978-1-911687-53-5
ISBN: 978-1-911687-58-0 (ebook)

Cover and page design: Caroline Li

THE
IDEAS
BOOK

60 WAYS TO GENERATE IDEAS
MORE EFFECTIVELY

KEVIN DUNCAN

MADRID | MEXICO CITY | LONDON
BUENOS AIRES | BOGOTA | SHANGHAI

FOR OTHER TITLES
IN THE SERIES...

CONCISE
ADVICE
LAB

SMALL BOOKS: BIG IDEAS

CLEVER CONTENT, DYNAMIC IDEAS, PRACTICAL
SOLUTIONS AND ENGAGING VISUALS –
A CATALYST TO INSPIRE NEW WAYS OF THINKING
AND PROBLEM-SOLVING IN A COMPLEX WORLD

conciseadvicelab.com

TO ROSANNA,
SHAUNAGH
AND SARAH.

CONTENTS

FOREWORD

The Canadian born journalist Malcolm Gladwell is responsible for popularizing a number of interesting ideas: in his breakthrough book, *The Tipping Point,* he got a whole generation of readers to appreciate the importance of social diffusion in what makes things popular. No matter that social science has largely disproved his interpretation of the literature on the subject. One fascinating by-product is the apparent legitimacy that *The Tipping Point* gives to "cool-hunting" – the practice of business hanging around with cool kids (mostly poor kids from deprived areas) to report back on their "influential" choices and preferences, hairstyles and sneaker choice.

In *Outliers*, he raises another interesting but contested idea from the dusty corridors of social science: the idea that to be a high performer – at music, sport or any similar skill-based practice – you need to spend 10,000 hours practicing. 10,000 hours is the magic number (and the title of one of the chapters in the book). Practice, as the adage goes, makes perfect.

This is an important and noteworthy idea because, as Anders Ericsson (Professor at the University of Colorado, the psychologist whose 1993 paper *The Role of Deliberate Practice in the Acquisition of Expert Performance* is the source of this idea) puts it, *"many characteristics once believed to reflect innate talent are actually the result of intense practice extended for a minimum of 10 years."*

The study Ericsson's work highlights is one by Berlin-based psychologists of violinists, but other writers – for example, Daniel Coyle and Gladwell himself – trace this notion in other contexts. Gladwell cites the importance of the Beatles' Hamburg residency in honing their skills as musicians and performers prior to their breakthrough. Others point to sports people as exemplars of a similar rule (the Arnold Palmer quote *"The more I practice, the luckier I get."* is widely touted by people discussing this in sporting contexts).

But is this all it takes to have great ideas? 10,000 hours of ideation (as our friends across the Atlantic call it)? Just have a lot and then you'll get some good ones?

Well, no. Not exactly.

For two reasons:

First, the 10,000 hours figure isn't as straightforward as you might think – in Ericsson's angry response to Gladwell he points out that 10,000 hours is the average, and that there is a range of scores either side of that mean figure. Many of the best performers in the study had "substantially fewer" hours of practice under their belts.

Second, the quality of practice turns out to be really important. It's not just any old practice – doing any old thing. You need to practice good routines and good ways of having ideas if you want to be a high performer in ideas.

Which is where Kevin's latest book comes in: this is like a training camp for people who want to have great ideas.

He's managed to boil down many of the essential tools and routines that help you to have good ideas. Some of which I've not come across before and some I realized to my own amusement I assumed were "natural" (i.e. they are routines I've now completely internalized).

Whether you're a beginner or a Grand Master, all YOU have to do is practice, practice, practice...

Mark Earls
Author of *Herd* and *Copy, Copy, Copy*

INTRODUCTION

The Ideas Book has become very popular and it's a pleasure to see that people get a lot of value out of these techniques.

Over the last 20 years I have trained many thousands, and they have all helped with their refinements to the material.

An idea doesn't travel unless it is explained well, and then 'sold' to whoever needs to approve or buy it.

International perspectives are particularly fascinating. It is a delight to have the book coming back in a range of languages – from Japan, China, and Korea to Germany, Spain, and Poland.

Good luck, and keep me posted on the blog.

Kevin Duncan
Westminster, 2022

PART ONE

PREPARING
TO GENERATE
IDEAS

A WORD ON...

PREPARING TO GENERATE IDEAS

Ideas suffer from two extremes:
not enough of them, and far too many.

It is possible that complete lack of imagination can
result in no ideas at all, but that is very unlikely.

It is also possible that an ideas session could
generate hundreds of ideas – all of them impractical,
unrealistic, or just plain useless.

The knack to generating a sensible number that can
genuinely be used lies mainly in the preparation.

Some of it is common sense, some of it involves
a bit of work, and most of it involves making some
tough decisions and standing your ground.

The simplest bad component – a horrible room or an
inappropriate attendee – can ruin the whole thing.

NOTE

Most of Part One applies to working with others, and in particular, to convening brainstorms. If you are working on your own, you could skip straight to Part Two, although some of the rigour behind the principle of 'brief yourself' may still apply.

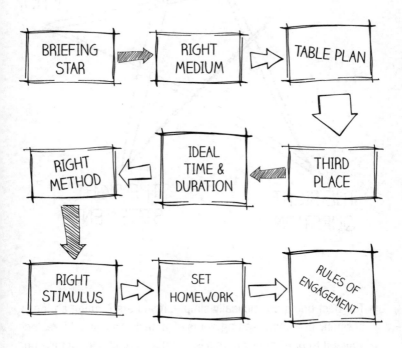

1. THE BRIEFING STAR

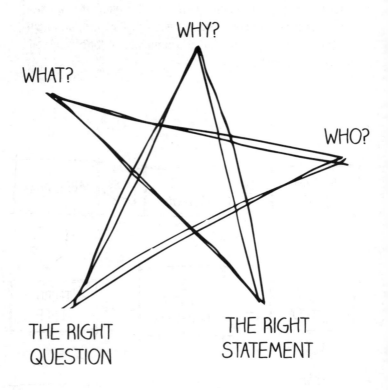

WHY?

WHAT?

WHO?

THE RIGHT
QUESTION

THE RIGHT
STATEMENT

✳ The best briefs are clinically simple. If you are running an ideas
session, or simply setting yourself a task, you should restrict
yourself to one sentence. This is worth spending a lot of time on,
because if it is not clear, no decent response will be forthcoming.

* Start with what? What are we trying to achieve?
* Then confirm the sense of that by asking why? Why are we trying to do this?
* If the answers are too vague or unsatisfactory, then change the what, or scrap the project altogether.
* Then describe the who? Who is this aimed at?
* The brief can now be expressed as a statement *(Our objective is to revolutionize the X category)*, or a question *(How do we double the size of Brand X?)*
* If the thinking is sufficiently clear and robust, it may be acceptable to have both an objective and a question: *Our objective is to revolutionize the X category. What single product feature would achieve this?*

EXERCISE

Choose a business issue that needs serious attention. Spend time articulating it in as short and clear a way as possible. First ask, what are we trying to achieve? Do not proceed until this is absolutely clear. If needed, ask the why question to cross check whether the what is sufficiently robust. Add the why. Experiment with using a statement as the brief, or a question, or both in tandem. Leave the result and come back to it later, make changes if necessary, then check with a respected colleague to see if they think it is a decent brief.

2. THE RIGHT MEDIUM

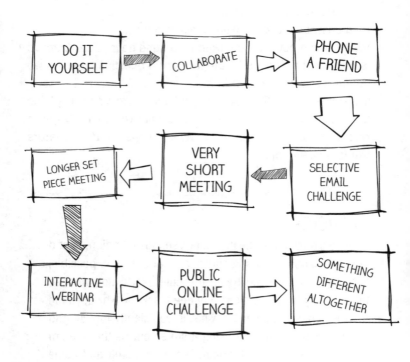

* Choosing the right medium in which to generate ideas is vital.
* Always start by asking *"Can I fix this myself?"* If the answer is yes, then don't go to all the bother of involving others. It will only be a huge waste of time for everybody, including you.

* Once you have decided that collaboration is necessary (not a decision to be taken lightly), then choose how best to issue the brief or challenge to someone else.
* First consider whether this could be just one individual. If so, only ask them. If you consider it unlikely, then choose how many others to ask (see 3. *The Table Plan*).
* Start simply: if you email the right number of suitable people a pithy one-sentence brief or question, are you likely to get back some excellent and inspired suggestions? In many companies, the answer is yes. This may generate an excellent response without the need for anyone to meet.
* If you decide meeting is necessary, then convene the shortest meeting in the world: *"Please come to Room X between 12.00 and 12.10, we will shout out a one-sentence issue, and you give us your instinctive response. We'll write it down and you can go."* If ten one-minute visits solve your problem, stop right there.
* If not, then move on to more public and time-consuming options.

EXERCISE

Choose an issue and work through the options in the box process. Consider the simplest, shortest route first in every case, and if it works, stop.

3. THE TABLE PLAN

* *"Anyone can have a great idea."* This politically correct mantra is completely wrong. Many people are not good at idea generation and should not be involved.

* *"When running a brainstorm, the more the merrier."* This notion is also false. The maximum number in any ideas session should be eight, and research shows that the optimum number is four.
* Even then, research also shows that individuals generate more relevant and inspired ideas when working on their own, so if in doubt, ask individuals to work on the brief on their own.
* If you have decided that you do need to convene a meeting, think very hard about who can come. Do not succumb to 'involving' or 'appeasing' people – the end result is always worse.
* Scrutinise every attendee for their relevance, skill, and ability to work with others in a productive and disciplined way. Design a table plan to suit.
* If they can't come, then do not accept a poor substitute – move the meeting so exactly the right people can come together.

EXERCISE

Scrutinize the brief. Interrogate the subject matter and work out who is best equipped to tackle the problem. Scan the entire company for suitable candidates. If they do not exist, look beyond the payroll to suppliers, partners, consultants, advisers, and others who could make a difference. Build the ideal team for the meeting and don't compromise if the logistics prove complicated.

4. THE THIRD PLACE TRIANGLE

OFFICE

HOME

THIRD PLACE

* Location and environment are crucial if you want to generate a decent idea. Being relaxed, sometimes even distracted, helps. The harder you force yourself to 'have an idea', the harder it can get.
* Barely anybody has generated a decent idea at work. And if they do at home it may mean they are working too hard.

* Analysis of great innovations shows that most were dreamt up in a 'third place', usually away from familiar surroundings. According to sociologist Ray Oldenburg, these are interactive environments where diverse talents gather, such as bars and coffee shops.
* So displacement from your normal environment is best when trying to come up with fresh ideas. Try to create these conditions.
* People think more freely in blue rooms, because it reminds them of unfettered landscape such as sky and sea. The higher the ceiling, the bigger the ideas.
* Natural light and fresh air are crucial – avoid dingy basements and sterile air-conditioned rooms at all costs.
* Or try wandering around outside – people think better when they are on the move (see 24. *Four Corner Walkabout*).
* If the subject demands it, make sure the right props relevant to the subject are available for use as stimulus (see 8. *The Right Stimulus*).

EXERCISE

Choose an environment that will inspire your guests. Consider energy levels, light, air, room for the mind to breathe, and interesting stimuli. What would be the ideal third place in which to conduct your session?

5. GOT THE RIGHT TIME?

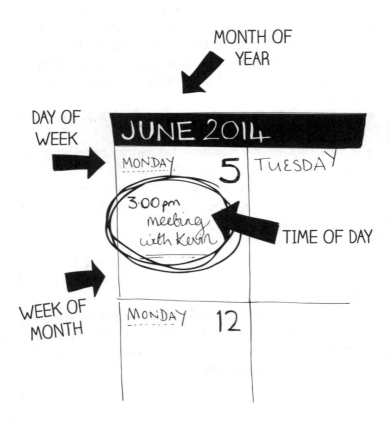

MONTH OF YEAR

DAY OF WEEK

JUNE 2014

MONDAY 5 TUESDAY

3·00 pm meeting with Kevin

TIME OF DAY

WEEK OF MONTH

MONDAY 12

✳ Don't just do a diary search, see when people can make it, and take that time slot. It may be completely counterproductive to the generation of good ideas.

* First, look as far ahead as possible, and ask when is the latest time the meeting can be held. If it is a long term project, avoid months when the attendees will be particularly distracted or under pressure (such as prime holiday time, budget planning rounds, financial year ends, and the end of sales cycle periods).
* Next, examine weekly patterns. Choose a week that carefully avoids pressure points, public holidays, company deadlines, and office events such as conferences.
* Now look at day of week. Avoid Monday mornings and Friday afternoons. Avoid set company rituals such as status meetings that always happen on a certain day.
* Then consider time of day. Few groups have inspired thoughts first thing in the morning or last thing at night. Choose a slot that fits the bill and stick to it.

EXERCISE

Spend five minutes considering all the worst times to hold your session and rule them out. Whittle your selection to an ideal week, day and time. See if your desired attendees are available. If not, choose the next slot with the same characteristics. Also consider whether the people in question are 'morning' or 'afternoon' people.

6. THE DURATION TIMELINE

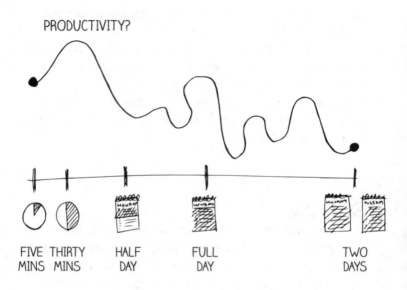

PRODUCTIVITY?

FIVE MINS THIRTY MINS HALF DAY FULL DAY TWO DAYS

* Duration is different from a moment in time. In business, absolutely everything is better when it's shorter. So your goal should be to organise the time it takes to generate ideas to be as short as possible.
* Time is a relative concept, so the definition of 'short' will be directly linked to the medium you have chosen (see 2: *The Right Medium*).

* An instinctive reaction to a task may only take a few minutes in a phone call, in response to a one-sentence email brief, or when popping your head round the door to answer a question. Aim for short wherever possible, so long as it solves your problem.
* People start to get bored in meetings after 30 minutes.
* Energy, attention levels and idea productivity start to dwindle as time elapses.
* If the complexity of the task, the personnel, the venue and the timing of the event can justify a longer time span such as a day, or even two, then think very carefully about how to pace it. Map out the meeting in minimum segments of 30 minutes, including regular breaks and injecting thought-provoking interventions and exercises regularly.

EXERCISE

Examine the task. First ask what the shortest possible duration might be in which it could be addressed. Imagine that's all the time you have. Now draw up a plan of how to use the time in the most productive way.

7. THE METHOD FLOW CHART

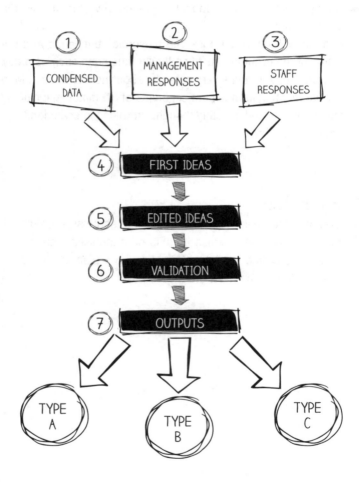

1. CONDENSED DATA
2. MANAGEMENT RESPONSES
3. STAFF RESPONSES
4. FIRST IDEAS
5. EDITED IDEAS
6. VALIDATION
7. OUTPUTS

TYPE A

TYPE B

TYPE C

* The most important point when choosing the right method is to have one at all. Far too many so-called brainstorms are convened without anyone running them properly, and with little or no forethought about what should happen when, and in what sequence.
* No matter what the duration, map out a sequence.
* In the example here, part one looks at all the available evidence. Part two examines the management view on the matter. Part three compares that with that of the staff. Part four outlines first ideas. They are then edited and validated, before being scrutinised for their most beneficial outputs.
* Allocate a disciplined time duration for each section.
* If you are struggling to generate a method, then select the most appropriate techniques in this book, and put them together in a logical order to reach a decision (remembering to put a time limit on each).

EXERCISE

Choose a realistic number of stages based on the task, the number of attendees, and the duration of the meeting. Sketch in what appear to be the most fruitful approaches, moving from explaining the challenge, to examining options, to generating new ideas, to whittling them to a manageable number, to a final decision.

8. THE RIGHT STIMULUS

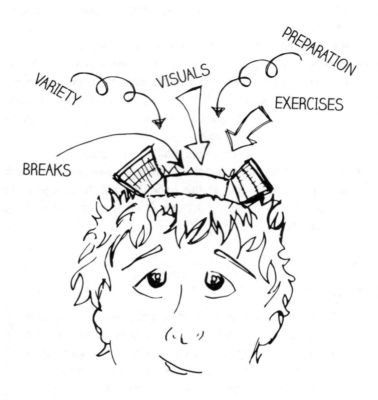

* Almost all ideas sessions are too long. The longer they are, the less productive they become.
* The onus is on the person running the session to break it down into the smallest possible chunks and ensure that the right stimulus is introduced at the right time.

* A maximum suggested run of time on one theme is 30 minutes. Some sections should be restricted to 5 minutes.
* Regular, disciplined breaks are vital.
* Variety keeps things fresh.
* Unexpected interventions keep the participants stimulated. If in doubt, have more of these in reserve than you may actually need.
* Exercises, practical application of what has been discussed, and group work can all lead to faster ideas, so long as they are not trivial or allowed to spiral out of control (either off brief, or for too long).
* This type of stimulus requires tight discipline, just like any effective facilitation, so the facilitator needs to take a firm grip on proceedings, and push people along.

EXERCISE

Look at your draft running order and imagine you were a guest at the session rather than the person running it. Imagine how fast you would get bored. Identify the pinch points at which boredom will set in. Choose these moments to introduce something unexpected. Use the ideas in this book to choose an appropriate number to stimulate the participants.

9. THE HOMEWORK CHECKLIST

BEFORE THE DAY:

1. READ THE BRIEF? ☐
2. READ BACKGROUND MATERIAL? ☐
3. HAD INITIAL THOUGHTS? ☐
4. READY FOR TEST AT START? ☐

* If you have looked at all the pages in Part One so far, your preparation should be almost complete.
* That's the preparation for the person running the session, but what about the attendees? Most people breeze into brainstorms and hope to improvise as they go along, but that does not lead to effective idea generation.

* As the organizer, consider carefully what homework you want to hand out well before the actual session. Working this out takes tremendous pressure off the session itself, and off you. The preparation of others is often as important as your own.
* Diligent attendees (which they should be since you handpicked them) will absorb the brief and all the background material before the day, thus avoiding the need for long-winded and often repetitive exchanges of information that eat into the time available and demoralise those who are diligent enough to be well prepared.
* For time-pressed or even evasive attendees, try telling them there will be a test on the briefing information at the beginning of the session, or ask them to present their best ideas at the start so they have to think in advance and then take ownership of their ideas in front of everyone else.

EXERCISE

Imagine that at the beginning of the session every attendee is brilliantly informed – they understand the challenge, the background, and are ready to come up with ideas. Now work backward and determine exactly what they would need in order to be at that level of understanding. Make sure they receive all that insight and information long before the session starts, with an appropriately firm instruction that it is essential that they prepare thoroughly.

10. THE RULES OF ENGAGEMENT

BREAK WITH THE PAST

PRODUCTIVE LISTENING

BREVITY = INTELLIGENCE

TAKE ISSUES SERIOUSLY,
BUT NOT YOURSELF

NO SHOW, NO SAY

NO JARGON

NO SHOWBOATING

NO CYNICS

* There is one final component that is conducive to great idea generation, and it is tonal rather than practical: the attitude of the attendees has to be right. And that means setting the right tone.
* Getting this right will depend on who you invite, their predisposed views on the subject matter, their mood on the day, and the manner in which you direct and control them.

* You can devise your own Rules of Engagement to reflect your company culture, but the main features should be common to most good working environments.
* To be strongly encouraged are: ignoring the past, productive listening, brevity, and a serious approach to the subject, but not to one's own ego.
* To be strongly resisted are: absenteeism (if you don't turn up, or are late, you should have no say in the decision), jargon of any kind, showing off or holding court, and cynicism.
* Be aware that there is a distinct difference between cynicism and pragmatism. Extremes are to be avoided in idea generation. Freewheeling, impractical ideas are as useless as the immediate killing off of every new suggestion.
* Finally, as we saw with the Third Place Triangle, try to create a relaxed mood. It leads to better ideas.

EXERCISE

If you are conducting an idea generation session, it is your job to set the tone. Plot the exercise from the moment you call it to your desired outcome. Review how you would like your participants to perform. Write down your expected behaviour, and make sure that all your communication about the job, including your performance on the day, reflects this.

PART TWO

GENERATING
INITIAL IDEAS

A WORD ON...

GENERATING INITIAL IDEAS

The debate surrounding whether anyone can
'be creative' or have a decent idea rages on.

One thing is clear: random, go mad,
"Give me your most whacky ideas, guys!"
approaches do not work well.

True creativity needs to be disciplined,
highly directed, and capable of
withstanding deep scrutiny.

In the absence of being brilliantly inspired
every moment of the day, most of us can
learn from the manner in which some
of the best ideas came about.

We can then try to recreate a facsimile
of those conditions to generate our own
more modest piece of mini-brilliance.

Start with the ideas in this part.

11. THREE GOOD, THREE BAD

GOOD

1 _____
2 _____
3 _____

BAD

1 _____
2 _____
3 _____

* Many idea sessions are derailed by negative material and attitude. It only takes one moaner and the whole thing can veer off in an unwanted direction.
* If you believe this is a possibility, then the *Three Good Three Bad* technique is excellent for combating it.

* Instead of allowing negative comment to creep in to proceedings, the technique deliberately seeks out the bad stuff, deals with it early, and offsets it with good stuff. This is sometimes called the car park - a place where all the negativity is parked.
* All attendees are asked to write down 3 bad things about the product/project/brief, and then 3 good. This draws the sting of all negative comment. They are not forced to generate three of each, but three is the maximum.
* The results are reviewed and summarized by the facilitator. Usually there is a significant overlap, and there is much to be learned about the degree of consensus, or an absolute focus on just one deficiency. It also shows how much the attendees really know about the subject.
* The exercise should always be done first, and should never last more than one hour, or 20% of the meeting time.
* All the good features are then used as inspiration to go on to provide an excellent solution.

EXERCISE

Think hard to work out if there appears to be an insurmountable problem with the brief, an unsatisfactory history to the project, a nasty constraint, or simply a prevailing culture of defeatism or cynicism. Use the technique to flush these issues out early and turn them into positive action.

12. THINK *INSIDE* THE BOX

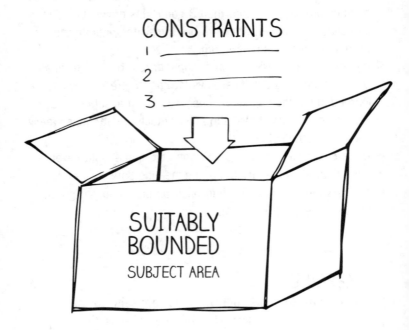

CONSTRAINTS

1 _____

2 _____

3 _____

SUITABLY
BOUNDED
SUBJECT AREA

* Thinking outside the box has been a trendy modern phrase supposedly synonymous with inspired lateral ideas.
* The problem is: it doesn't work.
* Most businesses have drawers full of eccentric, irrelevant, and sometimes downright stupid ideas that they can't use because they are commercially impossible, inappropriate, or simply off brief. Most were generated in poorly run brainstorms.

* In fact, the best creative ideas are generated when tight constraints are placed on the protagonists. They use the boundaries of what they can work with to be far more imaginative, and highly practical.
* This notion is thoroughly investigated in the excellent book *Inside the Box* by Boyd and Goldenberg.
* So in this technique, you should first map out all the constraints, so that everyone involved is fully aware of the boundaries of the subject area. You can do it before the day or at the start.
* This will force everyone to think harder and reduce the amount of fanciful, unusable material generated.
* The best example of this is in the film Apollo 13. After an explosion, the module's carbon dioxide filter is broken and the astronauts will suffocate. In Houston, the team head brings in three boxes containing everything available in the module. *"We need to find a way to make this,"* (holds up square filter) *"fit into a hole made for this,"* (holds up round one) *"using nothing but that..."* (spills box contents on table). They fix the problem.

EXERCISE

Examine the brief. Consider the most daft and unproductive areas that people might stray into, albeit with the best of intentions. Look at all the mundane practicalities such as price, production, distribution, timing, and resources – anything that could put a block on an idea. Use these parameters to define the 'box' inside which the idea needs to be generated.

13. EYES OF EXPERTS

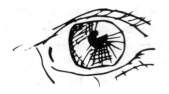 RICHARD BRANSON

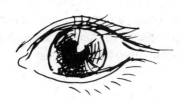 DAVID BECKHAM

 NELSON MANDELA

* This is a charming and fun technique that really works, regardless of the topic.
* The idea is to view the challenge through the eyes of a known person who is very successful at something.
* In this example, I have suggested a successful businessman, a sportsman, and a universally known political figure.
* It is not essential that they are technically expert, but it is important that they have a reputation for approaching their task in a distinctive way.
* The list of experts can be decided before the session, or generated spontaneously by the group (but do have some spares up your sleeve in case they choose all the usual suspects).
* Then examine the brief using the style and viewpoint of each expert. This can either be done collectively (all attendees imagining one expert at the same time), or separately (sending pairs or mini-groups off to work through the eyes of several different ones).
* Capture the ideas and vet them later in the meeting or after the session.

EXERCISE

Choose a list of respected experts. Work in turn through how you would imagine them approaching the brief. If David Beckham were working on this issue, how would he approach it?

14. CATEGORY STEALING

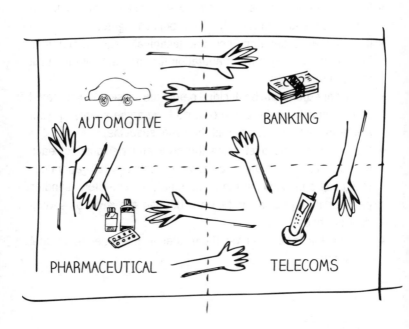

* The principle of *Category Stealing* is simple: choose a category different to your own and ask how they would approach your issue.
* Everyone operates in one category or another, and many of the traditions, rituals and formats in them operate in quite fixed ways. This can lead to sameness in one sector, but could provide inspiration in another.

* Start by listing a number of other categories. If you need reminding, scan the share prices in a newspaper, search online, or watch the TV for an evening. You will soon have an A-Z of categories.
* Identify the characteristics of well-defined ones, such as their usual approach to finance, branding, distribution, price, product features, and so on.
* Then work out what you can steal to apply to your brief.
* If a whole category doesn't have clearly defined traits, then take one brand instead that does. For example, how would Apple or Coke do this?
* If you work in a fairly obscure category, then look to the wisdom of well-known ones. If you work in a well-understood one, take the time to investigate more unusual ones. There is always something to learn.

EXERCISE
Choose three or four categories that are well removed from your own. Work out their main features and processes. Hone in on one brand in the category that is a particular success if necessary. Now imagine using that approach to grapple with your brief. Repeat for various categories as required.

15. PICTURE PLATFORMS

* *Picture Platforms* is great fun, and certainly not as trivial as it may first appear.
* Although the old adage that a picture is worth a thousand words may sometimes be disputed, there is no doubt that many people respond better to visual rather than verbal stimuli.

* In this technique, pictures are used as a springboard to new ideas about the brief. The pictures can come from any source - magazines, screen grabs, newspapers, books, catalogues, photo libraries, and so on.
* It is preferable if there is a wide range of styles - such as paintings, drawings, illustrations, colour, black and white – as well as photographs.
* If you require a specific and reasonably controlled response to the images, then choose a small number that are particularly provocative, reveal them one at a time, and ask for immediate ideas on each.
* If you prefer a more free-form approach, then offer a large set of images, and set the attendees running on the brief, allowing them to choose their own picture stimulus as they go along.
* Record all the ideas, and either group them on the spot, or edit after the session.

EXERCISE
Decide how many images you wish to offer as stimulus. If a low number (such as 10), then spend plenty of time selecting them. If a high number (100), then work out how you are going to allow the attendees to get at them. Cast the net wide, and make sure there is plenty of variety.

16. RANDOM WORD

* Random words take thoughts off into new and interesting areas.
* The words can be fairly obscure or seemingly irrelevant to the subject, so long as the resulting idea has a direct bearing on the brief. It will be your job as the facilitator of a session to set the boundaries.
* The words can be generated in all sorts of ways.

* Take a book. Ask someone to shout out a number – choose that page. Ask for another number – choose that line. Ask for a number between 1 and 10 – choose the word. Interrogate the word for all its possible applications in relation to the brief.
* Open a dictionary at a random page, close your eyes, and put your finger on a word. Get the attendees to do it to keep them involved.
* For more subject specific 'random' words, take a product specification, some material related to the product, or even your own brief, and put it through the software on wordle.net. Ask the attendees to stare at the result and suggest ideas.

EXERCISE

Choose your source of words based on the number of attendees, the amount of time you have allocated for the exercise, and the degree of interaction you require. If necessary, prepare some wordles based on relevant material. Consider how you are going to marshal the responses.

17. WHAT'S HOT?

SPORT

CURRENT EVENTS

POLITICS

CELEBRITY

TRENDS

* The truth is that products often have very little to differentiate themselves from their competitors.
* This could mean that there is not much very interesting to say about the product, and could mean that, no matter how hard you try to dig up something distinctive, there is very little forthcoming to go on.
* And that could mean a lacklustre brief.
* If that's the case, try *What's Hot?*
* This technique identifies current things that are interesting, and then looks for suitable ways to attach the brand to them. This needn't be cynical or exploitative. In fact, it is important that you do not accept a forced fit.
* Start by mapping out the most popular contemporary topics – celebrities, current affairs, events, trends, social phenomena, and so on.
* Choose a manageable number of these and exclude areas that have no discernible fit with the brief.
* Then work out how the brand can have a point of view on those issues.
* A word of warning: make sure that you are realistic about what your product can associate with – a stretch too far could be counterproductive.

EXERCISE

Identify half a dozen current hot topics. Use these to act as a backdrop to the brief. Generate ideas that will resonate more strongly in those contexts. If greater interaction is required, ask the attendees to identify what's hot before applying their minds to how that might help.

18. DIFFERENT LIGHT

* The *Different Light* technique is all about perspectives. We are who we are, and often it is extremely difficult to view an issue through a new lens.
* The further removed we are from understanding the target audience, the harder this could be.
* In many markets, the age of the decision makers is quite different from that of those buying the product. The best the marketers and designers can do is to listen to market research.
* This technique asks each attendee to abstract themselves from their normal viewpoint and pretend they are someone else. The more alien the role play, the more interesting the resulting ideas could be.
* Choose some unusual perspectives (in this example I have offered that of a child, a dog, an astronaut, and a refugee).
* As with many of these approaches, you can either apply one frame of mind to the whole group at the same time (in sequence), or can nominate different roles to different participants.

EXERCISE

Choose a manageable number of perspectives with which to view the brief in a different light. Decide whether you want everyone to adopt each role in turn, or if you will let them choose. Work through them and note down the most interesting ideas.

19. EXAGGERATION AND DEPRIVATION

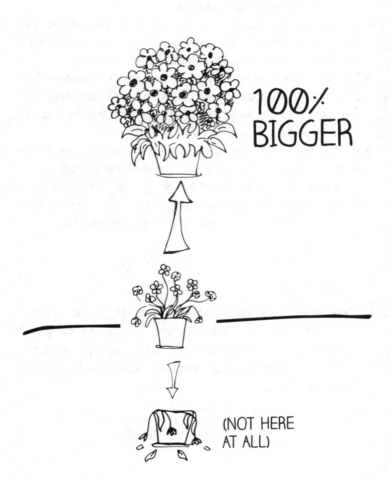

100%
BIGGER

(NOT HERE
AT ALL)

* As Goethe once enigmatically said, *"Everything has been thought of before, but the problem is to think of it again."* Although it's unlikely that he envisaged the iphone.
* The essence of this technique is to significantly over-exaggerate the benefits of a product, or push to ludicrous extremes what happens if it isn't present at all.
* Let's say a food product for kids has healthy ingredients, but is similar to those of competitors. Exaggerating the benefits of this to suggest superhuman powers, or the strength of an elephant, might lead to an interesting route.
* In the deprivation route, we envisage a world in which the product doesn't exist, thereby pointing out its vital role.
* Years ago Dunlop ran a commercial showing a couple playing tennis. Gradually all the things made by the company disappeared – the net, the court, the rackets, the ball, and finally their clothes. This elegantly showed the full range of their products.
* A similar hyperbolic route is to ask everyone for their worst possible idea, and use those to examine the extremes of the brief.

EXERCISE

Choose one product benefit. First, push to extremes via exaggeration what that benefit could be. Examine whether the hyperbole around the new thought leads somewhere interesting. Repeat for other benefits if helpful. Next, imagine what would happen if users were deprived of the product completely. Does that lead to a new way of expressing its value?

20. ANALOGY SPRINGBOARD

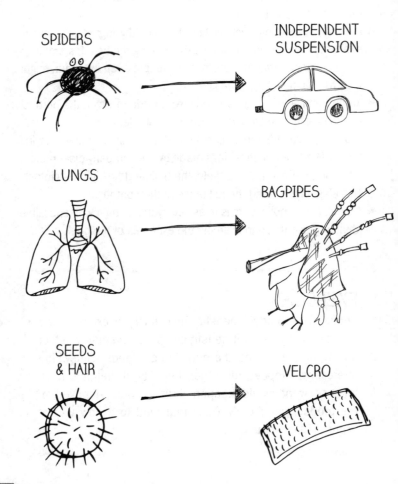

SPIDERS

INDEPENDENT SUSPENSION

LUNGS

BAGPIPES

SEEDS & HAIR

VELCRO

* Many of the best ideas in the world came from analogy – observing a phenomenon in one area of life and applying that idea to a totally different problem.
* The idea for Velcro arose when the inventor, Swiss engineer George de Mestral, took his dog for a walk and noticed how burrs (seeds) of the plant burdock stuck to the dog's fur. He replicated the idea to invent the product.
* Clarence Birdseye was on holiday in Canada when he saw some salmon that had naturally frozen in ice and then thawed. When cooked, they tasted completely fresh. This was the origin of the frozen food industry.
* An English designer called Cawardine approached the firm Herbert Terry in the 1930s proposing a desk light using the principles of the joints in the human arm. The Anglepoise light was born.
* Nature is one source, but there are analogies all around us.
* This is something of a freewheeling technique, and the possible sources of inspiration are effectively endless.

EXERCISE

Think of suitable stimulus with which to draw analogies to your brief. This could be as simple as thoroughly scrutinising all the objects in a room. If necessary, combine with the Picture Platforms or Random Words techniques in 15 and 16. Capture all the lateral thoughts generated.

PART THREE

DEVELOPING AND
UNDERSTANDING
IDEAS

A WORD ON...

DEVELOPING AND
UNDERSTANDING IDEAS

The ten approaches in the last part should be enough
to inject some variety into most ideas sessions.

But it is possible that you could try all of them on
a particularly thorny brief and still not come up with
a direction you are happy with.

So here are five more, followed by some techniques to help
you understand how the mind comes up with and reveals ideas.
Some are a bit more esoteric – deliberately so, since an obscure
angle could be precisely what is needed to unlock the problem.

The mind works best when it is relaxed.
Understanding how this works can remove the panic
that often sets in during the 'stumped' phase.
You can then work out how to nurture young ideas
sensitively, and begin elements of the editing process
that we will investigate more thoroughly in Part Four.

21. STICKING PLASTER SENTENCE

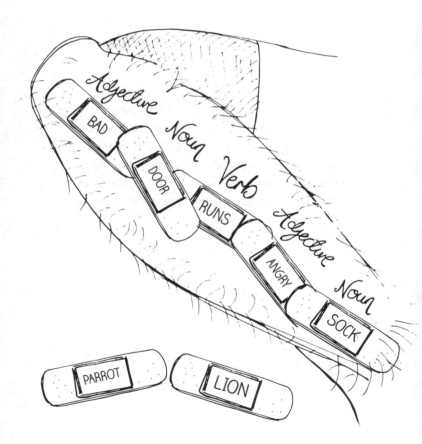

* We start this part with a rather weird idea – the *Sticking Plaster Sentence*.
* In Paris in 1925 a group of surrealist artists invented a game in which each person secretly thought of a word in the sequence adjective, noun, verb, adjective, noun.
* The first sentence they came up with was *"Le cadavre exquis boira le vin nouveau."* The exquisite corpse will drink the new wine. Quite.
* Pretty strange, I think you will agree, but then they were surrealists.
* In an ideas session, each component of the new sentence can then be used to interrogate the brief.
* So, for example, 'exquisite' and 'new' could lead to new descriptions of your product, 'corpse' could force the group to examine bodily benefits, and 'drink' might lead to a new look at customer consumption habits.
* Suspension of disbelief is required in this technique.
* Generate the adjectives, nouns, and verb in the correct sequence. The attendees can be asked to do it, or you can select them from reference sources in the same way as the *Random Word* example (16).

EXERCISE

Decide on a way of choosing the words – self-generated by the attendees or from reference material. Choose the number of sentences you want. Decide whether to generate them all at once and review them all together, or whether you want to scrutinize each one as it is revealed. Use the sentences to examine new perspectives on the brief.

22. CONCEPTUAL BLENDING

CONCEPT ONE

CONCEPT TWO

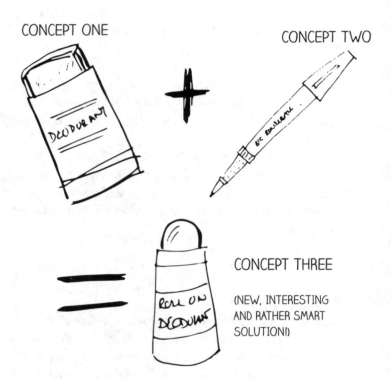

CONCEPT THREE

(NEW, INTERESTING
AND RATHER SMART
SOLUTION!)

✳ The light bulb has become a symbol or metaphor for having an
idea. The Spanish say *"Se me encendio la bombillo"* – literally
"My light bulb went on."

* Some of the best ideas come from taking an idea or concept and blending it with another to create a third one that is directly helpful to the new problem.
* The term *Conceptual Blending* was first coined by Jonah Lehrer in his book *Imagine*. This technique finds an overlap between seemingly unrelated thoughts – making separate ideas coexist in the mind is crucial to originality.
* Start with something we already know. In this case, it might be the brief itself, or a specific component of it.
* Then add or envisage something else we already know. This must be something that is unrelated to idea number one.
* Now blend the two together to develop a third idea.
* Example: 1. Deodorant. 2. Ball point pen. 3. Roll-on deodorant.
* Another example: 1. Beer 2. Mobile phone. 3. Pre-ordered drink at bar.

EXERCISE

Identify an idea or concept (this could be the brief, but may just be a product attribute). Decide how to generate a series of second, unrelated ideas, either through preparation or by getting the attendees to do it. Make sure you have plenty because you can't predict which combination the helpful third blended idea will come from. Examine all the third ideas to see what potential they have.

23. STRANGE OR FAMILIAR?

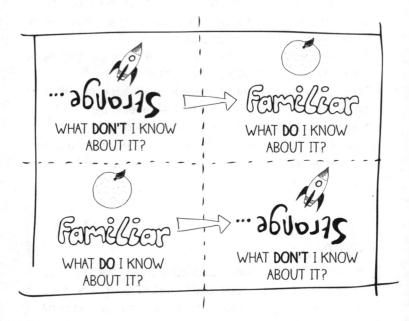

| Strange ...
WHAT **DON'T** I KNOW
ABOUT IT? | ⟶ | Familiar
WHAT **DO** I KNOW
ABOUT IT? |
| Familiar
WHAT **DO** I KNOW
ABOUT IT? | ⟶ | Strange ...
WHAT **DON'T** I KNOW
ABOUT IT? |

* This is a technique advocated by John Adair in his excellent book *The Art Of Creative Thinking*.
* We know that hitting upon an analogy of what the unknown idea might be like is a helpful step in discovering it. The reverse process – making the familiar strange – is equally useful to the creative thinker.

* There are two sides to this technique:
  1. Take something you find strange or hard to understand. How about a jet airplane? Work out what you do know about it, push to find out more, and then use what you have learned to develop ideas.
  2. Take something with which you are very familiar. How about an orange? Now interrogate it to work out what you don't know about it.
* Finding out more about something is logically beneficial. Making the familiar strange may sound counterintuitive, but in fact familiarity breeds conformity. In other words, we stop thinking about things we are familiar with – seeing them as odd, problematic or unsatisfactory reignites our curiosity and leads to better answers.
* Once you have grasped this technique and where it can lead, prepare a series of objects or topics to which you can apply it.

EXERCISE
Decide what familiar things you want to examine. This could well include your product or service, or aspects of it, or if not, then ordinary objects such as an orange or bottle. Now choose some strange things to investigate. Decide whether you want to do each in turn and capture ideas, or offer the full set to attendees so they can choose for themselves.

24. FOUR CORNER WALKABOUT

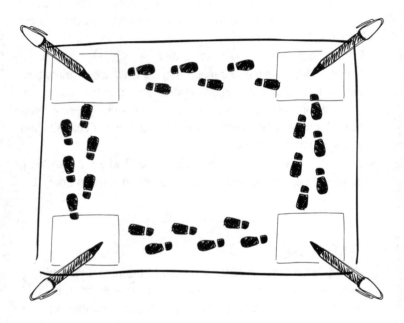

* This technique is easy and almost always surprising.
* One of its greatest assets is that it is dynamic and inevitably leads to interesting departures, but is always completely anchored in the brief.
* First, you need a room large enough to allow your participants to walk around. This may mean a big room, or you might want to re-arrange the furniture or remove a boardroom table.

* Then take four large sheets of flip chart paper.
* Choose four pivotal words from the brief, and write one only on each sheet.
* Place each sheet in a different corner of the room.
* Give your first attendee a marker pen, send them to a corner, and ask them to write the first thought they come up with next to the original word.
* They then move on to the next corner, and another attendee is sent to add to their thought.
* Keep sending everyone round, each building on what has gone before until each sheet is full.
* This technique achieves three things:
    1. Lateral departures that are intrinsically linked to the brief.
    2. Surprise and stimulation for the attendees when they see the ways in which their ideas can be built upon by others to generate something more powerful.
    3. People have better ideas when they are on the move.

EXERCISE
Choose four critical words from the brief. Write them on the sheets. Send the team round to add to them. When the sheets are full, review each in turn for new directions. If fruitful, choose four more words from those sheets, and repeat the exercise as often as necessary.

25. OUTLIERS

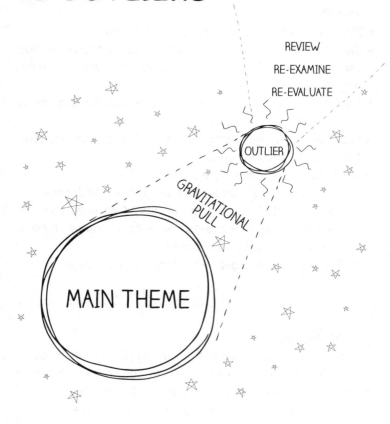

REVIEW

RE-EXAMINE

RE-EVALUATE

OUTLIER

GRAVITATIONAL PULL

MAIN THEME

* When it comes to having fresh ideas, the stuff at the edges is often the most interesting. That's why it pays to get all the familiar material off the table as fast as possible, freeing up time and energy to consider something truly new.

* In his book *Outliers*, Malcolm Gladwell points out that context is absolutely crucial – what appears to be a reason for something rarely is.
* This is a territory that Nassim Nicholas Taleb calls Extremistan. All the interesting stuff happens at the margin, he says, and a single outlier observation can have an inordinate impact.
* So, instead of concentrating on the consensus view at the centre of your brief, look to the edges for the outliers.
* What is the oddest thing about this brief/market/product /challenge?
* What appears to be a complete anomaly?
* Be highly quizzical about anything that is totally different from everything else. Review it. Re-examine it in a new light. Re-evaluate its possible relevance to the brief. Establish if there is any gravitational pull between it and the central issue.

EXERCISE

Identify the most odd outlier in the brief. Or ask the attendees to do it. Analyse it in intense detail to work out why it is where it is. Reassess your options based on this extreme perspective, and see if it sheds any new light on the possible answer to the brief.

26. THE UNCONCEALING

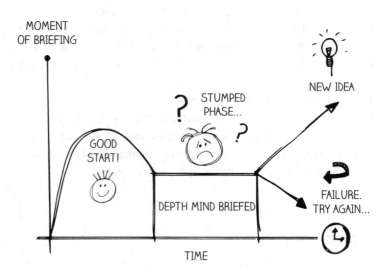

* How do you measure the imagination, or quantify an epiphany? New research has improved our understanding of this.
* Muses, higher powers and creative 'types' are myths – creativity is not a 'gift' that only some of us possess – it's a catch-all for a variety of distinct thought processes that we can all learn to use more effectively.
* Annoyingly, it's only after we've stopped searching for an answer that it often arrives.

* Breakthroughs often follow a *'stumped phase'* in which the brain has looked for answers but not found any.
* So, trying to force an insight can often actually prevent the insight – ideas usually arrive when the mind is distracted or allowed to relax. So, according to Jonah Lehrer, you should *focus on not being focused*.
* The brain has a short-term storage section (the prefrontal cortex), which is a working memory. This captures fleeting thoughts ready for joining together for a breakthrough.
* Ideas come from sheer persistence. If you work hard enough on something, there will eventually be an *unconcealing*, in which you 'suddenly' get it.

EXERCISE

First try any of the techniques in this book in a concentrated burst. If your efforts crack the problem, then great. If they don't, then withdraw and ignore the issue for a while. Your Depth Mind (see next) will already be briefed. Then, either wait for the unconcealing (which could happen to any team member when they least expect it), or reconvene the team again to revisit the issue.

27. TRAIN YOUR DEPTH MIND

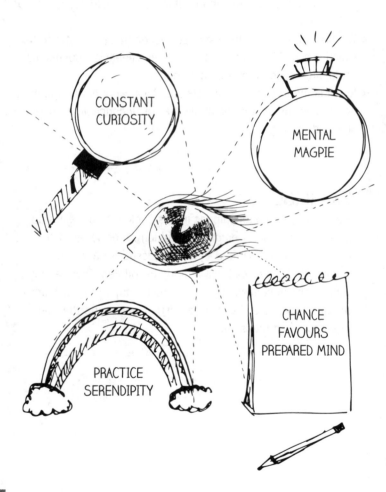

CONSTANT CURIOSITY

MENTAL MAGPIE

PRACTICE SERENDIPITY

CHANCE FAVOURS PREPARED MIND

* Making better use of your Depth Mind is an important skill for creative thinkers.
* Your Depth Mind is your sub-conscious. Once you have experienced an *unconcealing* – typically in a third place when you are quite relaxed and doing something else - then you can start to trust your Depth Mind to sort things out and generate solutions once you have 'briefed' it.
* But this doesn't just happen automatically. You need to train your Depth Mind and you can do that in various ways:
  1. Be constantly curious.
  2. Practice serendipity (the more you think, the more it appears you are in 'the right place at the right time').
  3. Become a Mental Magpie (collect stimuli often and from odd places).
  4. Widen your span of relevance (many inventions were conceived by those working in other fields, and, as the saying goes, chance favours the prepared mind).

EXERCISE

Examine the brief and then do nothing about it. Meanwhile, draw up a plan to deliberately expose your mind to some unusual non-work stimuli over the next few days. Create a system for capturing your observations about these unusual things. At the end of your off-duty period, examine those thoughts in the context of the brief. There may even be an Unconcealing before your review. If necessary, get colleagues to do the same.

28. PECKED TO DEATH BY DUCKS

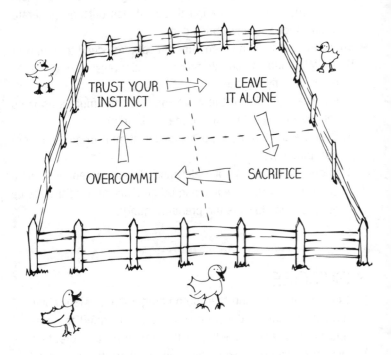

TRUST YOUR INSTINCT

LEAVE IT ALONE

OVERCOMMIT

SACRIFICE

* Here we combine the thinking of several experts to create a technique that attends to two sides of the same issue. *Pecked to death by ducks* is designed to:
  1. Allow an idea to flourish properly.
  2. Prevent it from being chipped away at before it has even got off the ground.

* Many companies (and individuals) have more creativity than they realise, but they inadvertently stifle it, or channel it in the wrong directions.
* There is a time and place for judging ideas, and we will cover this in detail in the next part. But in the embryonic phase, ideas should not be diluted until their full potential has been investigated.
* So, to avoid death by pecking, we subject the idea to four examinations:
  1. Trust your instinct: do you like it?
  2. Leave it alone: do not be tempted to fiddle with it.
  3. Sacrifice: what would you be prepared to sacrifice to make it happen?
  4. Overcommit: How could you devote every possible resource to it?
* These last two come from Adam Morgan in his book *Eating the Big Fish.*

EXERCISE

Pull together the best ideas you have so far. Subject them to the four-stage process, each idea in turn. If you suspect that any of the ideas have already been watered down, then go back to their original source and examine their unadulterated form. If necessary, reconvene the group to scrutinize the idea anew.

29. POST-IT VOTING

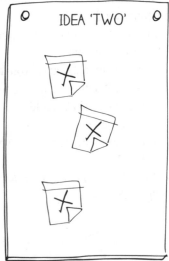

* With this arsenal of techniques, we really should be able to generate some excellent ideas to solve pretty much any brief.
* However, as the ideas start to flow, it is easy for sessions to become unruly, and one nasty consequence is that the attendees unintentionally spend far too much time on ideas that aren't in truth going to be very helpful. This is often not noticed amongst the enthusiasm and energy of the session.

* An excellent way to keep a regular handle on how productive the session is proving to be is to use the *Post-It Voting* technique.
* As soon as an idea is sufficiently articulated, capture it on a chart and stick it on a wall. As the session unfolds, the facilitator needs to assess either whether there are enough ideas to review, or if sufficient time has elapsed to justify a review.
* At this point, call a break for everyone else and, whilst they are smoking cigarettes or checking their mobiles, organise the material in a suitable format for review.
* When they come back in, give them all Post-It notes and ask them to vote for what they regard to be the most promising ideas.
* There are many variations to this. You can give them a limited number of votes (perhaps 3). You can ask for a rank order of 1, 2, 3 (using different note colours). Or you can just do it with pens.
* This allows you to eliminate unfruitful routes as you go along.

EXERCISE
Select a time period, or choose a quantity. When that moment is reached, call a break followed by a vote. Discuss the implications and move on. Repeat regularly.

30. KILL IT

IS THIS IDEA
REALLY
ANY GOOD?

* There is nothing worse than a protracted brainstorm in which a dead horse is being continually flogged.
* Although we have discussed the important principle of allowing new ideas to flourish and remain undiluted in their early life, there comes a time when a go/no go decision is needed.
* The *Kill It* technique may not be relevant in a session that is the very first on a certain brief. More likely it will be relevant on something that is reasonably long running, or based on an existing issue.
* The question is blunt and simple: is this idea really any good? The only two permissible answers are yes or no.
* Yes means go ahead and develop it.
* No means kill it now and stop wasting time.
* In large exploratory sessions, even if they are the first on that particular brief, there may be merit in issuing a limited number of *Kill It* cards (perhaps 3) to all the attendees.
* Like jokers in a game of cards, if a participant feels that an idea is so bad that it really needs to be killed immediately, then they can play that card. By doing so they will either trigger a robust and convincing defence of the idea, or prove that it is indeed poor and should be dropped.

EXERCISE

Take a series of ideas that have already been generated and call a review. Issue the Kill It cards and see how the material is culled. Anticipating a complicated session with many ideas, issue the cards before the meeting and explain the rules.

PART FOUR

JUDGING
IDEAS

A WORD ON...

JUDGING
IDEAS

The truth is that many people are incapable
of identifying an idea, let alone working out
whether it is good or bad.

Judging ideas tends to come 'naturally' to those
who have been involved with them all their lives,
typically in the creative industries.

Assuming we now have plenty of ideas, the next
challenge is to decide which ones to progress.

Most brainstorms generate far too many, and if the
number is too overwhelming then they simply lie
in a desk drawer – too daunting to tackle.

So this part is all about working out what merits further
development, and what doesn't. It is as important
to know what you are not going to do.

Here we take some of the most powerful constructs from
The Diagrams Book, and use them to judge ideas.

31. THE POTENTIAL PYRAMID

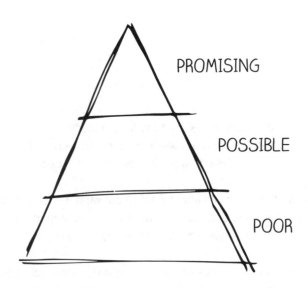

* *The Potential Pyramid* is very useful for grouping a large number of ideas into broad groups to get an initial feel for volume and potential.
* You can choose your own language, but for the purposes of this first sweep, I have selected promising, possible, and poor.
* Promising means that everyone agrees the idea has potential, albeit the details are unlikely to be clear yet. This doesn't matter.

* Possible means there are some reservations, but the view is that further investigation to prove/disprove potential would nevertheless be time well spent.
* Poor means there is significant doubt about whether to bother. Many ideas seem great when first generated, but on reflection they don't hold up under scrutiny.
* Write the number of ideas in each layer. If there is just one in the promising layer, this may be enough. If there are none, then look to the possible layer and be more specific about what to spend more time on.
* If there is enough potential in either of those, then drop everything in the bottom layer.

EXERCISE

Spread out all the ideas generated. What is the total number? How many each in the three categories? If there are no promising ones, look to the possible section. If there is enough potential in both top layers, discard all the rest and concentrate resource in the right place.

32. THE DECISION WEDGE

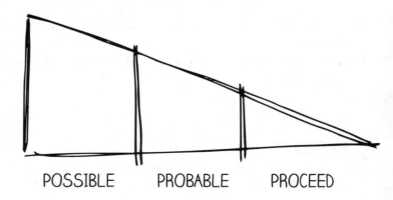

POSSIBLE   PROBABLE   PROCEED

* *The Decision Wedge* is a useful alternative way of looking at the merit of ideas.
* It can either be used after *The Potential Pyramid* has whittled out the poor concepts. Or it can used to overlay a more practical approach.
* So this technique analyses the ideas based not so much on their pure creative merit as on their practicality.
* The possible section should include all the ideas that could possibly be enacted.

* This is not however the same as the probable section, where the number is significantly reduced based on likelihood, and available resource, which will naturally be finite.
* The proceed section does not necessarily mean that the finished idea will see the light of day, but it does mean that at this early stage of judging, it is deemed sufficiently promising to proceed to the next development stage.
* It is important that the number of ideas in each section is entirely realistic for the company and the resources it has at its disposal.

EXERCISE

Take all the possible ideas and screen initially for practical possibility. Take a pause, or involve some new people in the process. Now judge for probability – likelihood of going ahead. Make sure the number in the proceed section is realistic.

33. THE JUDGING TRIANGLE

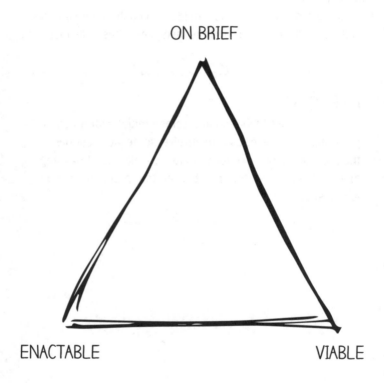

ON BRIEF

ENACTABLE

VIABLE

* *The Judging Triangle* provides a critical sense check for any idea.
* Is it on brief? If not, then go no further.
* Is it enactable? If it can't be done, then it doesn't count as a true idea.
* Is it viable? If the financial case is insufficient, then it is not going to benefit anyone.
* Unlike the Meatloaf song *Two Out Of Three Ain't Bad,* you need to be able to tick all three criteria with confidence in order to confirm that an idea is worth pursuing.

EXERCISE

Take each idea in turn and subject it to scrutiny. As soon as it fails any of the criteria, reject it, or change a fundamental part of it in order to make it acceptable.

34. THE ORIGINALITY PANE

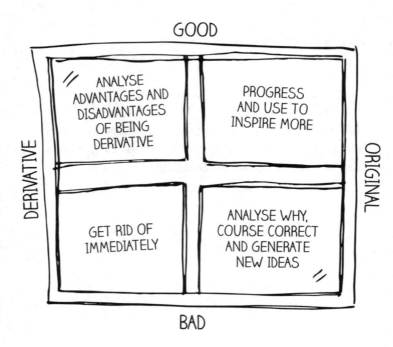

* This diagram helps to disentangle the good and bad elements of your ideas, and to examine the relative merits of being original or derivative.
* The vertical axis represents good at the top, and bad at the bottom.
* The horizontal axis represents derivative on the left, and original on the right.
* If you have several ideas in the 'good and original' segment, then there may be a case for simply developing those and ignoring the rest.
* Those in the 'good and derivative' section are not necessarily bad. Analyze the advantages and disadvantages of being derivative. Sometimes it is perfectly acceptable, for example in a market where those first in have made mistakes and passed on important lessons.
* 'Original and bad' ideas should probably be rejected, but may justify rapid examination to double check that they are beyond improvement.
* Anything in the 'derivative and bad' quadrant should probably be dropped immediately.

EXERCISE
Take a series of ideas. Work through them allocating each one to the relevant quadrant. If a healthy number reside in the 'good and original' box, then pursue them and reject the others. If not, work out what needs to be done to improve the remaining ideas.

35. THE IDEA RELEVANCE MAP

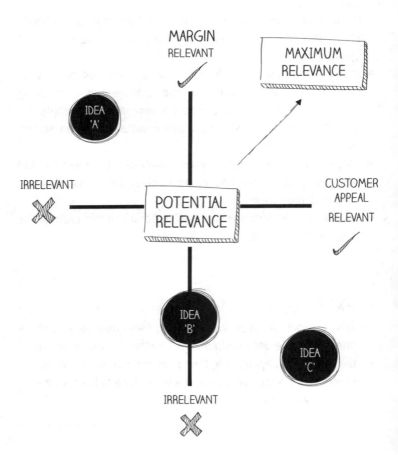

* *The Idea Relevance Map* is a very effective and highly flexible way to establish clarity when looking at any idea.
* It is particularly useful when a product or category has many different criteria that could determine the success or failure of an idea.
* Start by selecting two important variables that could establish the relevance of the idea. For example, try margin on one axis, and customer appeal on the other.
* Plot the two axes, always placing the highest relevance to the top right.
* Place the ideas in the appropriate spot on the grid.
* Repeat the exercise several times with different combinations of criteria, until all the important ones in the market have been covered.
* Ideas that consistently appear top right (in this case with the most relevant customer appeal and high margin) are those with the most potential.
* Those consistently appearing bottom left should be discarded.
* Those hovering somewhere in the middle may still have potential, but must be examined to see what can make them migrate to the top right quadrant.

EXERCISE

Identify the most important variables that could determine the relevance of an idea in your market or category. Work out how many maps that will require. Plot them, and add the ideas. Repeat as often as necessary to establish consistent winners, or what needs to be changed to improve relevance.

36. THE IDEA BRAVERY SCALE

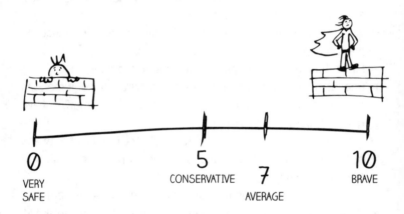

0
VERY
SAFE

5
CONSERVATIVE

7
AVERAGE

10
BRAVE

* *The Idea Bravery Scale* is a good way to establish how adventurous ideas should be before a lot of time and effort is spent enacting them.
* At first glance, many people think all ideas should be as brave as possible, but this is wrong. Plenty of companies actively dislike 'brave' things, particularly if their culture is inherently conservative.

* One school of thought also equates bravery to high risk.
* So to determine a suitable scale, you need to pose two questions:
  1. How adventurous is the company culture?
  2. Against that backdrop, how brave should the ideas be?
* A score out of ten is generated to see whether conservative (5-7), average (7) or brave (8-10) levels are desired.
* The scores can also be blended to create one overall figure. For example, a conservative company asking for brave ideas may need to have its scale weighted downward to reflect their overall conservatism.
* As the ideas come closer to being enacted, the scale helps to remind everyone involved what level of bravery was agreed, and provides a measure against which to compare.

EXERCISE
Pose the two questions. If the company culture is fairly conservative, then reduce expectation levels for the bravery of the ideas. Now score each idea using the scale, and work out which ideas are too brave, not brave enough, or just right.

37. THE CHANCE OF SUCCESS AXIS

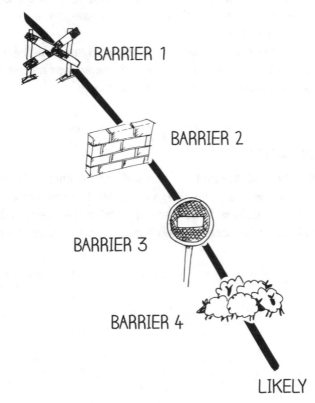

NOT LIKELY

BARRIER 1

BARRIER 2

BARRIER 3

BARRIER 4

LIKELY

* The degree of bravery in a company can be analysed in a different way.
* In the *Chance Of Success Axis*, each notch represents a barrier to action, in this case a series of reasons why the idea will never get off the ground. These could be practical, financial, or personal.
* Bear in mind that the personal barriers could be the most powerful in any company – perhaps a senior executive or committee that has the ability to block the idea.
* By mapping the decision-making process diagrammatically, each barrier to purchase can be identified and isolated.
* A plan to knock each one down can then be devised, or if the conclusion is that the idea will never be approved because there are too many barriers, then it can be abandoned.

EXERCISE

Choose an idea that you believe has merit. Use the axis to plot all the reasons that the company or executives in influential positions might have for not proceeding with it. If relevant, put the barriers to purchase in chronological order, or place the biggest or hardest ones first, to the far left. Then come up with a plan to knock down each barrier. If a barrier cannot be removed, you may have to admit defeat.

38. THE CENTRAL IDEA SATELLITE SYSTEM

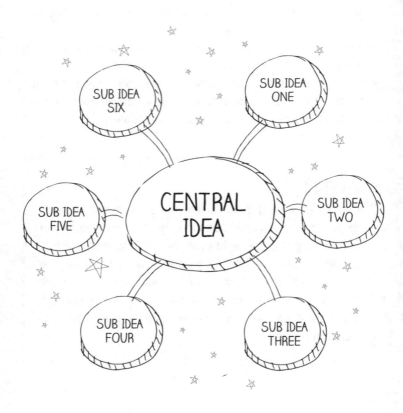

* Sometimes an idea isn't an idea on its own. Instead, it is interrelated with others, or has a number of sub-themes.
* If that is the case, then you can organise the various parts with *The Central Idea Satellite System*, which links them together in a layout reminiscent of satellites orbiting around a central planet.
* The hub of the idea sits in the centre, and is represented by the largest circle to denote its importance.
* Smaller satellites are then spun around it, normally a minimum of three and a suggested maximum of six. If there are less than three satellites, then the idea might not be as fertile as you first thought.
* Thematically the satellite ideas must be related to the central one.
* Use the diagram to explain the idea to others, and if necessary populate it with directional arrows to show what has an influence on what.

EXERCISE

Place the main idea in the centre of the system. Draw up a list of related sub-ideas. Arrange them in smaller bubbles around the central thought. If you run out of sub-ideas quite fast, review whether the central one is as full of potential as you originally thought. Otherwise, use the diagram to demonstrate to others the breadth and application of the main idea.

39. THE THREE BUCKETS

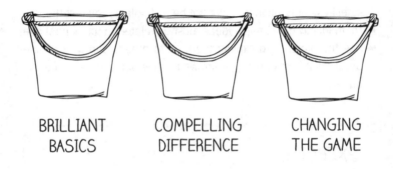

BRILLIANT
BASICS

COMPELLING
DIFFERENCE

CHANGING
THE GAME

* *The Three Buckets* exercise was introduced by Adam Morgan in his book *The Pirate Inside* in 2004.
* It is a very useful way to judge ideas and work out what role they might perform in the broader scheme of things.
* Each project must be placed in one of the three buckets.
* On the left is Brilliant Basics. These represent "excellence as standard." You or your company should be doing these well as a matter of course, just like your competitors.

* In the middle is Compelling Difference. These should be "significantly better than normal." These are demonstrably better than your competitors, but still not genuinely remarkable.
* On the right is Changing The Game. These are "truly extraordinary." They are utterly unique in the market, and genuinely remarkable.
* This exercise will reveal whether a large enough proportion of the ideas are going to make a genuine difference. If too many ideas fall in the left or middle buckets, or there are none at all on the right, then the ideas may not be good enough to progress.

EXERCISE

Take a list of all your ideas. Scrutinize them by the three sets of criteria and place them in the relevant bucket. Look at the quantity in each. Review whether the balance is right. Use the findings to cancel weak ideas or search for better ones.

40. THE PREMORTEM

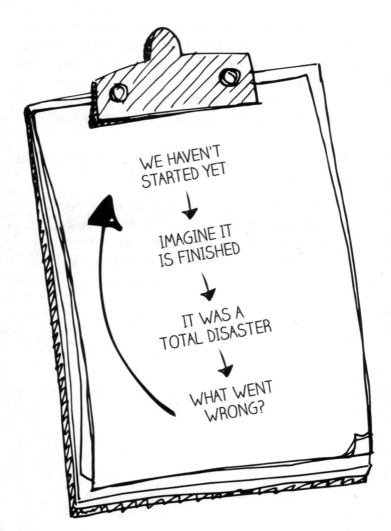

WE HAVEN'T STARTED YET

IMAGINE IT IS FINISHED

IT WAS A TOTAL DISASTER

WHAT WENT WRONG?

* Finally, *The Premortem* is a great way to run a final check to judge whether an idea is sufficiently worthy to proceed with.
* It was invented by Gary Klein and summarized by Daniel Kahneman in his book *Thinking, Fast and Slow*.
* The procedure is simple: when an organization has almost come to an important decision but has not formally committed itself, the decision makers gather for a brief session.
* They are asked to imagine that it is one year later and that the idea has been a complete disaster – they then have to write a short history of what happened.
* It is of course important that such a review is conducted long enough before it is too late and everyone is totally committed to proceeding.
* *The Premortem* could prevent many a disaster. By contrast, a postmortem may be useless.

EXERCISE

Articulate the idea. Draw up a list of the decision makers. Gather them for a short meeting. Ask them to imagine that it is one year in the future. Everything went ahead, but it was a disaster. Get them to write a short synopsis of what went wrong. Examine the results to see if the group has revealed a fatal flaw in the idea.

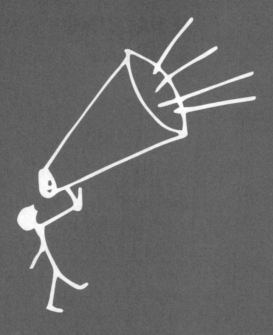

PART FIVE

ENACTING
IDEAS

A WORD ON...

ENACTING
IDEAS

Generating ideas may actually be the easy bit.

The world is full of people who had a 'great' idea,
but never made it happen.

So, enacting an idea may well be the hardest part.

Part of this is down to the commitment, energy
and enthusiasm of the person or team trying
to make it happen.

But it can also be down to the receptiveness
of colleagues, clients, customers, or even
entire companies.

So in this part, we look at the psychology
of how to increase the chances of an idea
actually being enacted.

41. THE MOTIVATION TRIANGLE

* Nothing gets done if no one can be bothered. And that means that motivation has to be effective, with everybody working at a consistently high level.
* That's easier said than done. In his book *Drive*, Daniel Pink boiled the essence of motivation down to three crucial elements.
* *Autonomy* is the desire to direct our own lives.
* *Mastery* is the urge to get better and better at something that matters.
* *Purpose* is the yearning to do what we do in the service of something larger than ourselves.
* The people involved in enacting an idea need ample quantities of these characteristics if there is to be a reasonable chance of it happening.
* Use *The Motivation Triangle* to work out if the team enacting the idea has the desire, the skill, and the sense of purpose to make it happen.

EXERCISE

Work out what really needs to happen to enact the idea. Consider if the team charged with doing it are sufficiently motivated. Ask in turn if they have the autonomy, mastery and purpose required to get the job done. If you think not, then work out how to equip and motivate them properly to have the strongest possible chance of success.

42. THE LIKELIHOOD OF HAPPENING PYRAMID

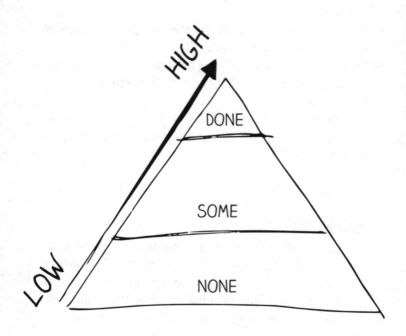

* *The Likelihood of Happening Pyramid* picks up from some of the ideas we looked at in the last part. It can help to determine whether this thing is going to get done or not.
* Start with one idea. Does it have a high or low chance of happening? If high, then do the simplest next thing to push it along. If low, then work out what needs to be addressed. If needed, use *The Chance of Success Axis* (37) to establish what the barriers are.
* Use the pyramid to determine resistance to action. If the likelihood of happening is 'none' for a single idea, then consider whether it is worth pursuing at all.
* If there are multiple ideas in the 'none' layer, then consider abandoning them.
* Examine the ideas in the 'some' layer to work out what needs to be done to make them happen.
* If you are using the pyramid to monitor many ideas, migrate completed ones to the 'done' level when they are completed.

EXERCISE
Choose an idea you wish to analyze, or a set of them. Use the pyramid to determine the likelihood of their happening. Put them in sequence from low to high, or from none to some to done. Add quantities if possible for each layer, and then choose your easiest segment as the place to start.

43. THE ADOPTION PREDICTION WEDGE

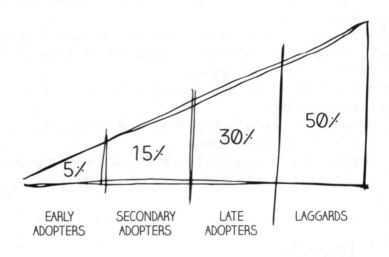

EARLY ADOPTERS · SECONDARY ADOPTERS · LATE ADOPTERS · LAGGARDS

5%   15%   30%   50%

TIME

* Enacting an idea doesn't always mean that everything has to happen at once. If you want to launch the complete package all at once, then maybe. But releasing an early prototype and then making refinements may be just as useful.
* *The Adoption Prediction Wedge* is a handy way of working out how much acceptance and adoption of the idea you really need to get underway. Sometimes if a few early adopters become fans, they can have a major bearing on future success.
* In this example, we examine the classic adoption sequence of a new product or craze. Early adopters are the first to get going, followed by the secondary and late adopters, followed at the end by the laggards.
* These sections are at their most powerful when populated by figures. If you can make estimates of adoption before proceeding, you may be able to make better decisions, or make a more convincing case to secure investment and commitment for the idea.

EXERCISE

Identify types of potential adopters or users of the idea, work out rough quantities of each, and plot them over time. Examine what these quantities mean for demand, supply, revenue, profit, company resource and other relevant factors. Use the prediction to plan the enactment of the idea sensibly, or explain the pace of it to any concerned parties who could affect its success.

44. THE IDEA PRIORITY MATRIX

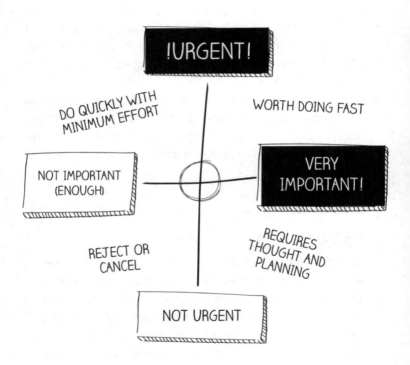

!URGENT!

DO QUICKLY WITH MINIMUM EFFORT

WORTH DOING FAST

NOT IMPORTANT (ENOUGH)

VERY IMPORTANT!

REJECT OR CANCEL

REQUIRES THOUGHT AND PLANNING

NOT URGENT

* *The Idea Priority Matrix* helps establish what order of priority you are going to give to all the ideas on your checklist.
* It can be applied to pretty much any time period - a day, a week, a month, or even a year.
* The vertical axis represents urgent/not urgent, and the horizontal one is very important/not important enough at the moment.
* If it is urgent and very important, then it is probably worth doing fast. The precise definition of 'fast' may vary. Start with today and put the tasks in priority order.
* If it is urgent but not important enough, then delegate it if you can, or do it quickly first using the minimum of effort.
* If it is very important but not urgent yet, think about what you need to do and plan when you are going to do it. Be sure to put this planned time into your diary immediately and stick to it when the time comes.
* If it is neither important nor urgent, then you should question why you are doing it at all. If possible, reject or cancel these ideas.

EXERCISE

Take your list of ideas. Choose a helpful time period, such as a day, week or month. Draw the diagram and place each idea in the appropriate quadrant. Methodically work through the action, starting with the most urgent. If relevant, use the matrix to communicate to all those involved why the order of priority is the way it is.

45. THE BOX PLANNING PROCESS

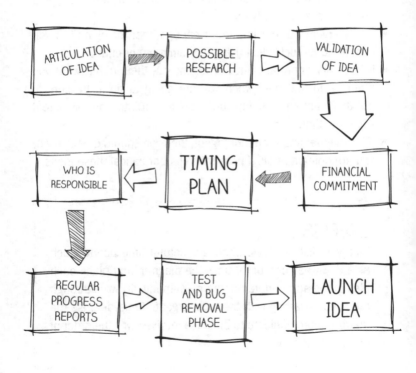

* *The Box Planning Process* enables you to work out how to enact the idea. It maps out everything that needs to be done, with each box containing a stage of work.
* The descriptions inside them should be short and clear, and durations can be added to each if helpful.
* Each stage is linked by a directional arrow that shows what happens next, and it is important that the sequence is accurate.
* In this example there are nine stages, moving from articulation of the idea, research and validation, through to financial commitment, responsibilities, progress reporting and testing.
* A cost per stage can be added to each box if it impresses the Finance Director or other investor.
* A well mapped out process like this allows the idea to transcend any criticisms of being 'too creative' or 'fluffy' by imbuing the whole thing with an organizational rigour.

EXERCISE

Take everything that is needed to make the idea happen, design a process, and break it down into stages. Place each stage in a box, make sure the sequence is correct, and link them with arrows. Make the descriptions as simple as possible. Add durations and costs per stage if helpful. Test-drive on a colleague to make sure all is clear.

46. THE RESPONSIBILITY CYCLE

1. WHAT?

2. WHY?

3. HOW?

4. WHO?

5. WHEN?

6. WHERE?

7. ARE WE THERE YET?

8. WHAT HAPPENED?

* Enacting something means that people have to take responsibility. They can only do this if they understand what's involved.
* *The Responsibility Cycle i*s an eight-point process to make sure that ideas and projects actually get done.
* Start with *What?* What are we doing here? Assuming this is satisfactorily answered, then the rationale is explained in the *Why?* section.
* The cycle moves on to ask how, when, and where the idea will be enacted, and crucially, who exactly will be doing what.
* Once all these elements have been thought through in a satisfactory way, the person or team responsible for making the idea happen needs to keep interested parties informed.
* *Are we there yet?* Requires a sensible mechanism for updating people on progress, and *What happened?* is the final report, or possibly even a postmortem.

EXERCISE

Choose an idea that needs to happen. Write down the eight questions. Answer each in sequence with a maximum of one sentence. If you cannot generate a satisfactory answer to a question, do not continue with the others. Instead consider how to get round the problem, or whether to abandon or rethink the entire idea.

47. THE ANNOUNCEMENT CIRCLE

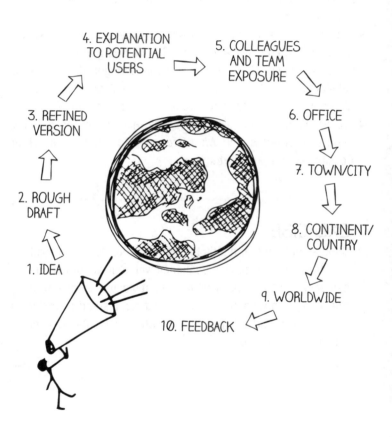

4. EXPLANATION TO POTENTIAL USERS

5. COLLEAGUES AND TEAM EXPOSURE

3. REFINED VERSION

6. OFFICE

2. ROUGH DRAFT

7. TOWN/CITY

1. IDEA

8. CONTINENT/COUNTRY

9. WORLDWIDE

10. FEEDBACK

* There is no point in having a brilliant idea if no one knows about it. This could refer equally to colleagues as it could to potential customers.
* *The Announcement Circle* helps to map out how the idea will find its way from the drawing board to the wider world.
* Start by generating a rough draft of the idea in a form that most people would easily understand. If the subject matter is quite specialist or technical, refine different versions for different audiences, and then try explaining them to potential users, and/ or relevant colleagues.
* Once you are satisfied that the message is clear, you can widen the announcement, moving outward in scale to the whole office, various cities, overseas, or even worldwide.
* Use feedback at any stage to refine the message.
* Plot all this before starting, and attach timing and who is responsible to each stage.

EXERCISE

Look at the current articulation of the idea. Now consider every possible audience that may need to understand it. Generate as many different versions of the announcement as required to satisfy them all. Now plot the most effective sequence in which to reveal it all. If necessary, use the plan to give others confidence that the launch has been well constructed.

48. THE PANIC EARLY LINE

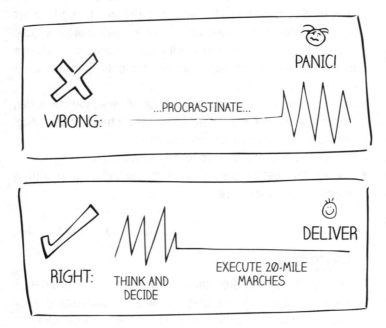

* *The Panic Early Line* encapsulates the fact that most people (and companies) leave things too late before they start enacting an idea.
* For most people this was a habit they acquired at college when faced with a deadline for handing in an essay or dissertation.
* This timeline helps to focus the mind on the task ahead while there is still plenty of time.

* The right way to do it is to examine as much of the material and as many of the important issues as early as possible. It is vital at this point that all the decision makers are present to set direction with full authority.
* Once direction is decided, then orderly execution of the work can be embarked on, with completion being achieved smoothly.
* This can be done by a series of 20-mile marches - a concept introduced by Collins and Hansen in their book *Great By Choice*.
* They explain that Amundsen beat Scott to the pole by consistently marching 20 miles a day. In bad weather he did it anyway, and in good he stopped at 20 to save energy for the next day. Scott's team either stayed in their tents on bad days or overshot and wore themselves out on good days, reducing their energy for the next day.
* Jobs get done best using consistency. Map out the right amount of effort for the right timespan.

EXERCISE

Choose an idea that needs to be enacted. Work out who needs to be involved in order to complete it, and convene a meeting with them as fast as possible. Decide direction in that meeting, and announce it to everyone else that needs to know. Then map out which 20-mile marches need to occur to make it happen smoothly.

49. THE PHASED ENACTMENT PLAN

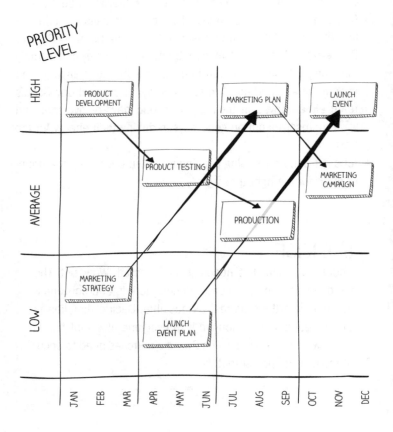

* Sometimes ideas are highly complex, and require a long time to come to fruition. In this example, let's say it will take a year from conception to launch.
* This will mean there is a huge amount to do, and lots to be coordinated. As a result, it is not realistic for every aspect to be top priority all the time.
* *The Phased Enactment Plan* maps this out in simple ways so everyone knows what they are doing and when.
* Start by creating a vertical axis and choosing a scale of priority. In this example, I have chosen high, average and low, but this could equally be a 1-10 scale, or 0-100%.
* Now plot the various stages that need to happen, and put them in the right chronological order. Take a reasonable guess about how long each stage will take.
* The crucial final part is to determine the priority level. This will undoubtedly change during the course of the project.
* In this example we cover product development and production, marketing, and a launch event. If there are too many variables, then produce a separate enactment plan for each discipline.

EXERCISE

Determine the vital elements of the project. Draw up a plan and choose a suitable priority scale and time period. Try plotting all the elements on one plan. If the result is too confusing, then create separate plans for each element.

50. THE IDEA ENERGY LINE

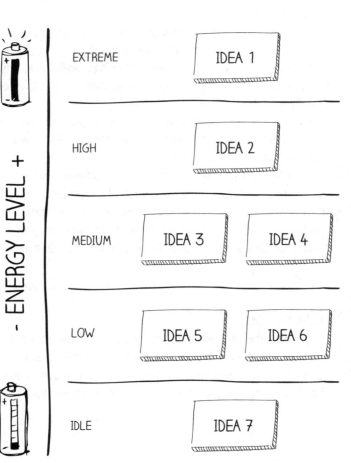

ENERGY LEVEL + / -

EXTREME — IDEA 1

HIGH — IDEA 2

MEDIUM — IDEA 3   IDEA 4

LOW — IDEA 5   IDEA 6

IDLE — IDEA 7

* And finally, an idea inspired by Scott Belsky from his book *Making Ideas Happen.*
* Most companies (and individuals) have far too many projects on the go at once, and as such their most precious commodity is energy. They only have a finite amount of it and can't do everything at the same time.
* *The Idea Energy Line* requires you to map out how much energy each idea should receive.
* It is important to note that this categorisation is not based on how much time you are spending on a project – the emphasis is on how much energy is being expended at any given moment.
* Classifying your ideas in this way prompts questions about the degree to which you are focusing on the right ones.

EXERCISE

Draw up a list of all your ideas. Place each one in one of the energy categories, from extreme to idle. Remember to concentrate on energy level, not time spent. Move them around until the priority is right. Repeat the process as often as is necessary depending on the number and average duration of the projects. If the result is daunting, consider dropping some of the less important ideas, or concentrating on a shorter time span.

PART SIX

EXPLAINING
AND SELLING
IDEAS

A WORD ON...

EXPLAINING AND SELLING IDEAS

Some people are good at coming up with ideas, but not very good at explaining them to others. If they make a poor job of that, then the idea is not 'sold'.

Selling an idea means that it will be approved, whether by a boss, a budget holder or a customer.

So, you need to be able to take your point of view or idea, explain it well and sell it to the decision-maker.

The key to doing this successfully is having an excellent line of argument.

You should map this out and make sure the sequence is persuasive and comprehensive.

This part explains how.

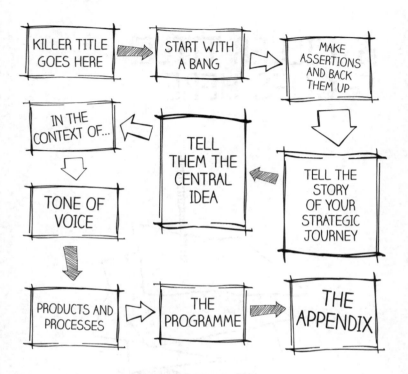

NOTE

The best way to map out an excellent line of argument is to get a large piece of paper, preferably no smaller than A3. If you have access to sticky notes, make each individual point you want to make on a separate note, and stick it in the right place on the larger sheet. Keep pushing this around until the argument you lay out is logical and coherent. Follow the suggestions in this section for advice on how to populate each box. To download free printouts, visit **theideasbook.net**

51. KILLER TITLE GOES HERE

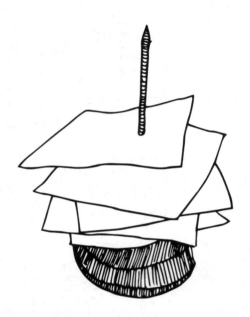

* Start by writing down your best shot at a killer title. It may be a bit weak at first, but make sure you get it down.
* Make it truly reflect the main point you are trying to get across.
* It must be accurate and engaging. Accurate means that it truly reflects what you are proposing. Engaging means that it captures the audience's imagination.

* If you are presenting something unusual or unexpected you might want to write a provocative question, such as: 'Why is this idea X better than alternative Y?'
* If you are trying to persuade your audience of a particular stance, then you could state: 'Idea X: An essential element of our success next year'.
* If you want to generate emotion, put it in before the subject matter: 'Touching peoples' lives: The Power of Idea X'.
* Do not write 'Presentation to X' and put the date on it. This is a wasted opportunity.
* Play around with the chosen title and constantly check it against the content of your proposal as it develops. There is nothing wrong with changing the title once you have written down your case, as long as it is an improvement.
* On no account select an image from a photo library and use that as your starting point.

EXERCISE

Scratch out your best attempt at what you are trying to say. Find different ways to make it evocative and appealing. Use it to anchor your thinking, and then work through the steps in this part of the book. Keep checking back against the title, and improve or adjust it as your case develops.

52. START WITH A BANG

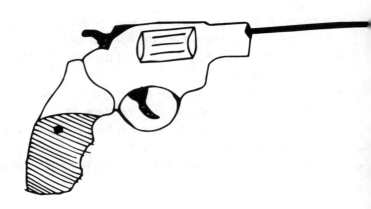

* In public speaking training, attendees are often encouraged to use a grabber. A grabber is a first spoken point or a visual that grabs the attention of the audience.
* One way to do this is to start with a controversial statement. This could well be something that you expect the audience to disagree with – a starting point for a debate that you intend to conclude satisfactorily.
* A dramatic way to grab attention is to state the opposite of what you will eventually be proposing.
* Number guessing games are also engaging: write a figure on a chart (preferably a high number) and ask the audience what it refers to.

* A milder approach is to start with a quotation that sums up the dilemma, or provides an interesting perspective on it.
* Whatever you do, do not repeat the brief or cut and paste 'the task' or 'the objectives'. This is lazy and adds no drama to what the audience already knows.

EXERCISE

There are many audience types. Different groups and individuals are drawn to:

Results: Don't bore with details. Deliver snappy points. Talk 'results'.

Emotions: Show genuine interest in feelings. Give help & support.

Abracadabra: Give it some magic. Make it interesting and sparky.

Data: Make research, facts and figures perfectly precise.

You need to read your audience and grab them with something interesting at the start.

53. MAKE ASSERTIONS AND BACK THEM UP

* Explaining an idea and getting people to agree with you involves making assertions, and backing them up.
* One without the other doesn't work.
* Assertions on their own can be refuted simply by saying: "I don't agree."

* Facts and logic on their own, without an opinion attached, are boring and not persuasive.
* So, you need to challenge assumptions and be brave, with backup.
* Re-express the issues intelligently. Don't hide negatives in a list of things to do – be honest about the severity and complexity of the job.
* Then follow with solutions that solve the problem.
* Show data and evidence that support your argument.
* If suitable, cross-fertilize knowledge from different disciplines and show the breadth of your thinking.

EXERCISE

Work out how many claims or assertions you wish to make. Can you justify them? If you believe so, then marshal the proof to back up what you are suggesting. If you have no backup, then consider dropping the point. One strong point is better than several weaker ones.

54. TELL THE STORY OF YOUR STRATEGIC JOURNEY

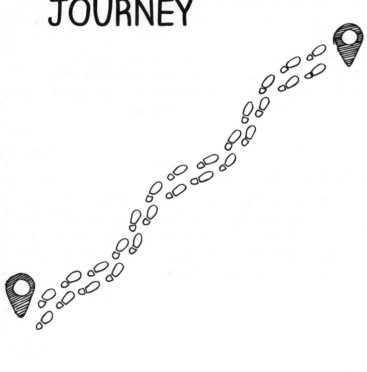

* To persuade someone to agree with you, you can't just arrive at the end and expect them to say yes. You need to take them on the same journey of thinking that you have been through.
* It's a bit like a maths exam, where you are asked to solve an equation. You can't just say the answer is 6.3 – you have to explain your workings.

* Start broadly, explaining that you looked at many options first and then whittled these down to a manageable number, such as three or four.
* Then examine those in much more detail, explaining what you investigated, and where it led. Explain any cul-de-sacs you reached.
* Don't reveal the answer yet. Tell the story first so that the audience knows you have looked at the whole thing properly.

EXERCISE

Work back through all your thinking at the beginning of the task or project. Write down all the options you investigated. Include all the possible answers that didn't work – dead ends, prototypes that didn't work, maths that didn't add up, unoriginal thinking, and so on. Now weave all that into a story, explaining your most powerful points in an engaging sequence.

55. TELL THEM THE CENTRAL IDEA

* This is where you reveal your idea: "So, I propose we do X ..."
* If you are presenting on behalf of a team or department, be sure to use 'we' to make it clear that you are not taking all the glory.
* Find a creative expression of what 'X' is, and how it will come to life for the product, brand or company.

* You may want to point out that this is such a fertile idea that it works effectively for a range of audiences, vertical markets, countries, channels, and so on. Demonstrate some examples of this.
* For example, you might say: "We have cherry-picked six ideas from the implementation programme to demonstrate the point, and they are..."
* If it is a large showcase presentation, you could bring some examples to life using video, personality endorsements, graphics, and so on.
* To sum it all up, consider using a distinctive diagram or a crystal clear sentence that your mum could understand.
* For more detail on this, look at page 90.

EXERCISE

Try pitching on a postcard. Can you express what you are proposing in one short sentence or paragraph? If not, your proposal may be too long-winded or confusing.

56. IN THE CONTEXT OF...

* One of the easiest criticisms of any proposal is that it is too narrow in perspective. A classic easy rebuttal will sound something like: "Of course, you don't understand the bigger picture..."
* So, don't just dive straight into the details of your favourite topic.
* Instead, review their whole strategy and plan in a wider context.
* Reference all the options and show how your proposal fits in with the total plan or picture. That might be the total company or department strategy, a range of products, a phased plan throughout the year, or something similarly big.

* This prevents you from being labelled as a narrow specialist and increases the chances of the audience agreeing with you, assuming your understanding of the bigger picture is indeed accurate.

EXERCISE

Consider how and where your idea fits 'in the context of' the bigger picture. Work out whether you want to explain the idea first, and then put it into context, or whether it might be better to describe the context first and then slot your idea into it.

57. TONE OF VOICE

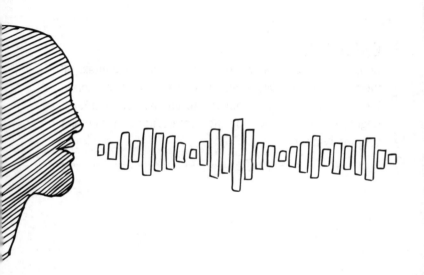

* Don't confuse what you wish to say with how you wish to say it. It is perfectly possible to tell the same story in many different ways.
* Start by selecting no more than three adjectives that reflect the right tone of voice you wish to convey. Cross-check your choice with the nature of the audience, as in the exercise in 52 ('Start with a bang').
* Try to choose words that you have not seen in business documents before – they are usually standard stuff that is full of cliché.

* Go back through the proposal and see if it is on brief for the tone you wish to convey.
* Make changes as necessary and then rehearse to see if you like the way it comes across.

EXERCISE

Look at your company culture. Look at the nature of your audience. Consider their personal style(s). Work out what sort of tone will increase the chances of them agreeing to your idea. Now write the proposal in that style, or use a mixture of styles to cover several audience types.

58. PRODUCTS AND PROCESSES

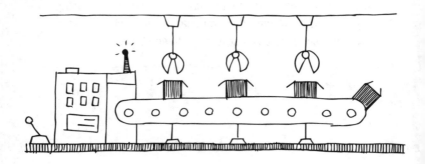

* Most companies have some kind of products and processes that they are trying to sell to customers. Sometimes departments are trying to sell these to their own colleagues and bosses.
* The problem is that these products and processes are not usually very interesting in their own right. It's the problem they solve that is of interest.

* Too many presentations start mentioning all this stuff at the beginning, and it is rarely interesting. It is only when all the issues have been explained that the products and processes have a place.
* If they do, now is the time to introduce them as clever solutions to tricky problems – but only if they are relevant.
* Try to demonstrate their efficacy by reference to success elsewhere: "We introduced X to situation Y and look at the results."

EXERCISE

List out any products and processes that you want to propose. Then ask: Are they relevant to this task or project, or are you merely suggesting them because they happen to exist? Next, look at the sequence. Have you mentioned them far too early, before identifying the issues that need addressing? If so, move them right to the end, and position them as a solution to a problem that you have articulated well.

59. THE PROGRAMME

* You are now clear to outline the specific programme or plan that you are recommending to implement your idea.
* Most people like to see this on one page only, but beware of cramming too much operational detail onto a single chart. In presentation form it may be too hard to read, and even in a document this can make the reader switch off.

* If necessary, break it down into smaller manageable chunks, but not too many.
* Summarize the hygiene factors, such as costs and resources, as succinctly as possible.
* If at all possible, put all the extra detail in the appendix (see next section); don't present it when you are first trying to persuade someone of the merit of your idea.

EXERCISE

Take one sheet of paper and map out the proposal in the simplest possible way. Don't get bogged down in operational detail. Does it clearly explain what you are proposing? Try it out on a colleague for a couple of minutes and see if it makes sense. Make changes and only then decide how to portray it on a computer.

60. THE APPENDIX

* The appendix is your great friend. It is where all the detail goes that would ruin the flow of the main proposal if it were included there.
* Too much information can distract everyone and interrupt your story.

* So, put all backup material in the appendix. Don't 'protest too much' in the main line of argument by providing too much evidence.
* Don't stray into this material if the job is done.
* In other words, if they agree with your recommendation, don't use it at all.

EXERCISE

Grab a highlighter pen and go through your proposal. There are two approaches here:

1. Highlight only the most effective and relevant points. Relegate anything else to the appendix.
2. Highlight all the technical detail that isn't relevant to the main point and move it to the appendix.

APPENDIX
DIAGRAM SOURCES AND FURTHER READING

4, 22, 26. *Imagine,* Jonah Lehrer (Canongate, 2012)

12. *Inside The Box,* Boyd & Goldenberg (Profile, 2013)
   The Accidental Creative, Todd Henry (Portfolio Penguin, 2011)

13, 16, 17, 19, 21, 22. *Flicking Your Creative Switch,* Wayne Lotherington (John Wiley, 2003)

20, 23, 27. *The Art Of Creative Thinking,* John Adair (Kogan Page, 1990)

24. *Where Good Ideas Come From,* Steven Johnson (Penguin, 2010)

25. *Outliers,* Malcolm Gladwell (Little Brown, 2008)
   Antifragile, Nassim Nicholas Taleb (Allen Lane, 2012)

28. *Eating The Big Fish,* Adam Morgan (John Wiley, 1999)

39. *The Pirate Inside,* Adam Morgan (John Wiley, 2004)

40. *Thinking, Fast and Slow,* Daniel Kahneman (Allen Lane, 2011)

41. *Drive,* Daniel Pink (Canongate, 2009)

48. *Great By Choice,* Collins & Hansen (2011)

50. *Making Ideas Happen,* Scott Belsky (Portfolio, 2010)

More detail and examples can be found in the following books:

Run Your Own Business, Kevin Duncan (Hodder & Stoughton, 2010)

Small Business Survival, Kevin Duncan (Hodder & Stoughton, 2010)

So What?, Kevin Duncan (Capstone, 2008)

The Diagrams Book, Kevin Duncan (LID, 2013)

Tick Achieve, Kevin Duncan (Capstone, 2008)

For one-page summaries of over 350 business books, visit **greatesthitsblog.com**

A NOTE ON DIAGRAM 'DUPLICATION'

Fans of *The Diagrams Book* will notice that a number of the diagrams in this book are the same as those in the previous book, but populated with different information. I make no apology for this. The knack with good diagrams is not so much to invent brand new ones all the time, but to find new uses for effective ones, using new circumstances.

THANKS FOR COMMENT

Ant Hill, Carmen Marrero, Katy Clarkson, Laura Robinson, Stuart Butler, Tim Rich.

ABOUT THE AUTHOR

KEVIN DUNCAN is a business adviser, marketing expert, motivational speaker and author. After 20 years in advertising, he has spent the last 22 as an independent troubleshooter, advising companies on how to change their businesses for the better.

CONTACT THE AUTHOR FOR ADVICE AND TRAINING:
kevinduncanexpertadvice@gmail.com
expertadviceonline.com
theideasbook.net

ALSO BY THE AUTHOR IN THE *CONCISE ADVICE* SERIES:
The Bullshit-Free Book
The Business Bullshit Book
The Diagrams Book
The Excellence Book
The Intelligent Work Book
The Smart Strategy Book
The Smart Thinking Book